THE POWER OF 10%

HOW SMALL CHANGES
CAN MAKE A **BIG** DIFFERENCE

Table of Contents

Sometimes

it's the smallest decisions

that can change your

life forever.

~Keri Russell

Introduction

Nothing will ever be attempted
if all possible objections must be
first overcome.

~Samuel Johnson

I'm never going to learn this new technology...
so why even make the effort?

Our team will never be the top performer...
so why even worry about improving at all?

I can't give anything close to what they need...
so why give at all?

I don't have much extra time...
so how can I possibly make a difference?

I can't solve the world's problems...
so why even try?

**If you've ever had any thoughts like these,
then you're reading the right book!**

What would happen if...

you improved your golf score by *10%*?

you exercised *10%* more?

you invested *10%* of your income?

you spent *10%* more time with your family?

you spent *10%* more time on your personal development?

you gave *10%* more often to those in need?

you did *10%* more to go after your goals?

Then...

you could go from being an "o.k." golfer to a "great" golfer.

your health and quality of life could improve.

you would have a significant nest egg for retirement.

you and your whole family would benefit.

you could enhance your job performance and your career.

you would bless others through the collective efforts of many.

you would find that, over time, you could achieve the unimaginable.

Great things are not

done by impulse,

but by a series

of small things

brought together.

~Vincent van Gogh

To improve ourselves, we do not need to
tackle everything all at once.

In fact, expecting a 100% total transformation is unrealistic and will set us up for failure. We will get much greater results by concentrating on small areas since all aspects of our lives are connected.

Have you ever woken up late and left home in a hurry only to find yourself playing catch up all day long? While we certainly have the ability to choose our thoughts, many times, once we wake up on the wrong side of the bed, it's difficult to get ourselves out of this rut. On the opposite side of the spectrum, have you ever started an exercise program only to find that those once enticing sweet treats no longer have the same appeal? After all, why spend all of that time exercising and then continue to eat poorly? In addition, you may then begin to make different choices about how you spend your leisure time: choosing to take an after dinner walk rather than splurging for dessert. It is nearly impossible to make a change in one area of our lives without this change influencing some other area.

If we focus on making targeted 10% improvements, we will find that other areas in our lives will be positively impacted as well. It is this collective strength, this momentum, that underlies *The Power of 10%*.

Good actions give
strength to ourselves
and inspire good actions
in others.

~Plato

The choices we make, the words we say,

and the actions we take not only

impact our lives, but also the lives of those around us.

With six billion people on this planet, we unavoidably interact with, influence, and impact the lives of others on a daily basis. Just as the moon affects the tide; the rain affects the crops; and the tilt of the earth's axis affects temperature, we cannot help but to affect the lives of those around us.

When you aim to improve yourself, remember that your changes will inevitably inspire others to improve. Your organization's enhancements will likely encourage other organizations to upgrade. And the betterment of one society will often influence other societies to become better. Whether on an individual, organizational, or societal scale, it is clear that *no man is an island.*

Contained within the following chapters you'll find inspiration to go after your dreams, whether through our ideas and examples or stories of others who have made great strides with respect to improving themselves, their organizations, or society as a whole. Often, the original ideas were quite small yet, over time, the power of 10% allowed mighty transformations to take place.

We hope that after reading this book, you will see the potential in any given moment, realize how the small things really do matter, and have the confidence to unleash...

The Power of 10%

Do something wonderful,
people may imitate it.

~Albert Schweitzer

Applying
The Power of 10% to...

Commitment

Never doubt that a small group of thoughtful, committed citizens can change the world; indeed, it's the only thing that ever has.

~Margaret Mead

Committed...
To a cause.
To making a difference.
To improving lives.

In 1942, Clarence Jordan founded Koinonia Farm, a small farming community outside of Americus, Georgia. On this Southern farm, which promoted fellowship among all, blacks and whites were paid equally and everyone was invited to sit at the dinner table, regardless of color. Because these beliefs were radical at the time, Koinonia's members were forced to deal with death threats, firebombs, property damage, KKK rallies, and economic boycotts. Yet the farm and its members, committed to their cause, survived.

In 1965, Millard and Linda Fuller first visited the farm. Three years later, they permanently moved to the farm and together with Clarence Jordan developed the idea of "partnership housing" — using volunteer labor to build affordable housing for those in need. The Fullers then went on to spend three years in Zaire (now the Democratic Republic of Congo) where they established a successful house building program.

THE POWER OF 10%

It was in 1976 that the Fullers founded Habitat for Humanity International. This organization, which former U.S. President Bill Clinton called "the most successful continuous community service project in the history of the United States," has built more than 250,000 houses, sheltering more than 1,000,000 people in more than 3,000 communities worldwide.

By one group enduring difficulties, remaining focused on the mission, and being committed to their cause, one idea, which began on a small Southern farm, has truly impacted countless lives.

When commitment combines with the power of 10%, we can see a world transformed. People, committed to a cause, form an idea, which produces the spark, which inspires individuals, which grows to impact others, which in turn inspires even more...

Commit to your goals. Commit to your passions. Commit to your beliefs — 10% more. It's clear that the world may be improved through the committed focus of individuals — through the power of 10%.

Unless commitment is made, there are only promises and hopes; but no plans.

~Peter F. Drucker

My satisfaction comes from my commitment

to advancing a better world.

~Faye Wattleton

THE POWER OF 10%

Integrity

It is curious that physical courage should be so common in the world and moral courage so rare.

~Mark Twain

Integrity: *Doing the right thing*

Taking the high road

Acting according to one's values

We *expect* to find examples of integrity from teachers and coaches, pastors and parents, leaders and mentors; within schools and churches and other places where values are taught. Yet, one of the best examples of integrity can be found in the business arena, from a former professional athlete. This was rather unexpected.

In 1977, Roger Staubach, the NFL Hall of Fame quarterback for the Dallas Cowboys, Heisman Trophy recipient, and MVP in Super Bowl VI started The Staubach Company. This real estate service firm's legacy will last for generations.

The Staubach Company adheres to five core values, the first being *integrity*. As evidence that Roger Staubach *walks the talk*, he invites customers to adjust his fee if they aren't happy with the company's services. While it's rare that he issues a refund, Staubach offers this guarantee as proof of his company's integrity. The client, not the commission, is the number one responsibility.

This exemplary service to the customer also extends to his employees. Staubach says, "You have to treat your people with integrity if you expect them to treat customers the same way." Employees are encouraged to live balanced lives outside the office by volunteering in the community or leaving early to attend children's activities. He says that letting employees have that balance allows them to "work harder for you and believe in your organization."

Here is one man who truly characterizes *integrity* through his beliefs, words, and actions. Through the power of 10%, this one value becomes magnified and permeates not only his life, but his company, the lives of his clients and employees, and the lives of those with whom *they* interact. Allow your integrity to radiate and positively influence the world around you.

Choose to take the road less traveled.

The path may be bumpier,

the landscape plainer,

the duration longer.

But the destination will truly be

worth the journey.

THE POWER OF 10%

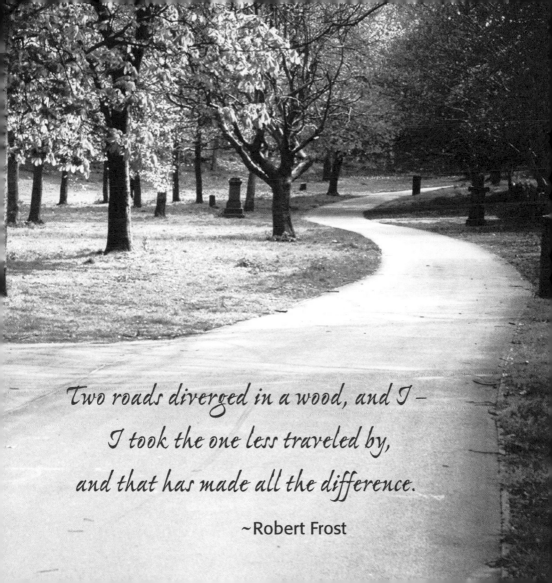

Two roads diverged in a wood, and I –
I took the one less traveled by,
and that has made all the difference.

~Robert Frost

Perseverance

Continuous effort

– not strength or intelligence –

is the key to unlocking our potential.

~Winston Churchill

She was in the middle of a divorce. Her career was at a stand-still. Ten years earlier, a car accident nearly took her life and her body remained compromised. Yet, she ran.

It all began when a friend came over, noticed her spirits were down, and suggested that they go for a jog. "I didn't know what I was doing. I didn't have the right clothing or jogging shoes. But I went along, because I didn't know any better," she remembers. "All I knew was that my life was crumbling and my method of coping wasn't working. I needed something else."

That first evening, Carol Henry jogged two miles. "Two miles! Are you kidding me? We jogged two miles? How did that happen?" At the end of the night, after she commented profusely about how amazed she was to jog such a long distance, her friend suggested that they train for a 5K. "A 5K, what's that?" Carol remembers asking.

During this tumultuous time in her life, her friend would come by every evening and they would jog. Carol looked forward to the daily runs. Day by day, week by week, they increased their distance...by 10%. Slowly but surely...

With persistence.
With passion.
With perseverance.

The two friends raced in a 5K, then a 10K, and eventually ran a marathon. Carol even ran her second marathon the following year. The process became so rewarding that she decided, *If I can do this, then maybe I can become a counselor and help others through their difficulties*. With the same tenacity, she began taking classes to get her Masters in Psychology. One class at a time. Slowly but surely...

With persistence.
With passion.
With perseverance.

What began as a distraction from the burdens of life led her to where she is now. As a licensed professional counselor and licensed marriage and family therapist, Carol now has a thriving counseling practice. She persevered through her darkest days and, through the power of 10%, not only improved her own life but the lives of hundreds of individuals.

It is natural to want to quit when things are difficult. Fear of failure, disappointment with reality, or anger over what we *wish* would happen can keep us paralyzed from taking action. Sir Isaac Newton's first law of motion is, in very simple terms, *a body in motion tends to remain in motion and a body at rest tends to remain at rest.* When we are "at rest" we do not feel like pushing forward. So, many times, we don't. What we often forget is that *motivation* does not always come first. Many times, it is action that must take place first.

Once we begin to move forward, we gain traction, and then feel encouraged, and then become motivated to proceed. Eventually, we look back and realize how far we've come. Staying in motion and persevering through difficulties, even though we don't *feel* like it at first, is the key to tackling life's challenges. Push forward, persevere, and you'll see how that first 10% step of action can lead you to accomplish your wildest dreams.

Persist and persevere, and you will find most things that are attainable, possible.

~Lord Chesterfield

Just remember, you can do anything you set your mind to, but it takes action, perseverance, and facing your fears.

~Gillian Anderson

Optimism

Optimism:

—noun
a disposition or tendency to look on the
more favorable side of events or conditions
and to expect the most favorable outcome.

One committed optimist inspired generations. As a child, she had every reason *not* to be optimistic. She was unable to hear, unable to see, and unable to speak. In the early 1880s, many believed that the future for Helen Keller, who had become blind and deaf when she was nineteen months old, was hopeless. Yet it was her optimism, as well as the optimism of her parents and beloved teacher, which allowed her to conquer her physical handicaps and inspire the world.

In her autobiography, *The Story of My Life*, Helen recalled that Anne Sullivan — her teacher — came and *set her spirit free*. With Anne's help, Helen Keller learned to speak, read, and write. In 1904, she graduated from Radcliffe College becoming the first deaf-blind person to earn a Bachelor of Arts degree.

Her optimistic outlook allowed her to break free from the confines of her physical limitations and reach out to the world around her. A champion for the underdog, Helen was an advocate for social causes, such as women's suffrage and workers' rights. She devoted her working life to The American Foundation for the Blind and founded The Helen Keller Institute.

So strong was her belief in optimism that she even wrote a book titled *Optimism*. It was in this book that she wrote, "No pessimist ever discovered the secrets of the stars, or sailed to an uncharted land, or opened a new heaven to the human spirit."

The ubiquitous Helen Keller,
who for many has become a symbol of optimism,
left a legacy of inspiration, resilience, and hope.

Optimists have been known for being more successful, forming stronger social networks, and living longer than pessimists. This makes sense. An optimist has a sense of hope that, in the end, things will work out. The dream will be achieved, the goal will be accomplished, the task completed. With this outlook, an obstacle isn't viewed as an insurmountable impasse, but rather a smaller bump only momentarily obscuring the positive outcome from sight. This viewpoint gives the optimist the ability to have lower levels of stress hormones, reach out to friends in times of need, and keep pressing forward when things don't go as planned.

Choose to look on the more favorable side of things — 10% more often. Choose to press forward, even when all the odds seem stacked against you — just 10% more. Your choices will not only help you, but will allow you to inspire optimism in others, through the power of 10%.

For myself I am an optimist –

it does not seem to be much use being anything else.

~Sir Winston Churchill

Optimism is the faith that leads
to achievement.
Nothing can be done
without hope and confidence.

~Helen Keller

Time

He was the 15th of 17 children,

born the son of a poor candlemaker.

He had a little more than a year of formal schooling.

He became an author and editor;

scientist and inventor;

statesman and diplomat.

He was Benjamin Franklin.

Benjamin Franklin was a great optimist, a visionary, a forward thinker. In his will, he left 1,000 pounds sterling each to the cities of Boston and Philadelphia.

"I wish to be useful even after my death, if possible,
in forming and advancing other young men,
that may be serviceable to their country
in both these towns."

He specified that the money was to be used to make low-interest loans for young apprentices. One hundred years after his death, after the money had grown considerably, only part could be disbursed. It was this money that helped to create The Franklin Institute of Philadelphia and The Benjamin Franklin Institute of Technology. His additional stipulation was that the remaining money couldn't be distributed for another 100 years. In 1990, 200 years after his death, the money was worth $6.5 million. What began with a fairly small sum turned into an immense monetary amount, capable of influencing the lives of countless individuals. And it all began because of one man's small philanthropic act.

*The most powerful force in the universe
is compound interest.*

~Albert Einstein

Greatness Takes Time

While life in the twenty-first century brings unprecedented efficiency, it also brings an overwhelming urgency. This lifestyle makes it easy to forget that *greatness takes time*. We want everything in the here and now – right here, right now. With improvements in technology occurring daily, it only makes sense that we feel entitled to have things immediately. And when frustrations mount when life isn't happening fast enough, it's nice to bring a little humor into the equation. The late George Carlin once said, "When someone is impatient and says, 'I haven't got all day,' I always wonder, *How can that be? How can you not have all day?*"

Truly magnificent structures, natural wonders, and rare marvels are only here because of the power of 10% – because of small changes taking place over time. Over time, the Colorado River has carved one of the world's most impressive examples of erosion: The Grand Canyon. This canyon is 277 river miles long. At its deepest, from rim to river, the canyon is over one vertical mile. In some places, the canyon, rim to rim, is 18 miles wide. What we see now is the result of centuries upon centuries of work. Look also at the pearl.

What was once a mere piece of sand within the folds of the mollusk, with the power of 10%, becomes a precious gemstone. Beginning with a small action, little by little, the power of 10% has produced sights which are truly impressive to behold.

Begin today to invest 10% more time in those things that are important to you. The dividends you'll receive will be worth the wait. Remember: Whether eroding rock or growing money, *greatness takes time.*

Life is all about timing ...
the unreachable becomes reachable,
the unavailable become available,
the unattainable ... attainable.
Have the patience, wait it out.
It's all about timing.

~Stacey Charter

The best time to plant a tree
is twenty years ago.
The second best time is now.

~Proverb

Love

To do something, however small,

to make others happier and better,

is the highest ambition, the most elevating hope,

which can inspire a human being.

~John Lubbock

She loved the color blue and the color purple.

She loved making stuff and designing clothes.

She loved penguins and her kitten Herbert.

She loved helping others by raising money

to find cures for pediatric cancers...

And she was loved by many.

Alexandra "Alex" Scott was diagnosed with neuroblastoma, a childhood cancer, shortly before her first birthday. While receiving a stem cell transplant when she was four years old, Alex told her mom, "When I get out of the hospital I want to have a lemonade stand." She wanted to give the money to the doctors to help them find a cure for childhood cancer.

Later that year, Alex held her first lemonade stand and raised $2,000. As Alex continued to hold yearly stands in her front yard, news of her love and dedication to her cause spread. People held their own lemonade stands and donated the proceeds to *Alex's Lemonade Stand Foundation*. Over time, her story became known and people all over the world began to fall in love with Alex. She was interviewed on The Oprah Show, The Today Show, CBS Early Show, and by Good Housekeeping Magazine. Her story was featured in hundreds of newspapers and on radio and television stations.

In 2004, at the age of 8, Alex passed away. During her short, but precious, existence she had raised over $1 million to help find a cure for the disease that took her life.

Her love for her cause – and her love for other children battling cancer – gave her the strength to make a difference and to inspire others to do the same. By 2008, *Alex's Lemonade Stand Foundation* had raised over $20 million for childhood cancer research. Lives all over the world have been, and will continue to be, affected because of the love inspired by one dear, remarkable little girl.

Allow the love for those things that you hold dear
to inspire you to get involved, to support one another,
to make a difference.

Reach out 10% more often
and take action while you can.

Our moments in life may be fleeting but, in the end,
the good that we can achieve, through love, remains.

I love you

Not only for what you are

But for what I am

When I am with you.

~Roy Croft

We can do no great things;

only small things with great love.

~Mother Teresa

Creativity

Creativity is the power to connect the seemingly unconnected.

~William Plomer

He was a man of action.
He was committed to his community.
All he needed was the right challenge.

When the professor gave the assignment to "come up with a way to improve the environment," Matt Cooper remembered an earlier conversation he had with a fellow classmate. His friend was concerned that edible, slightly aged produce was being thrown away from local grocery stores, while people in the community were going hungry. To her, this didn't seem right. But, *that was the way it was.* To Matt, this seemed like the perfect challenge.

After weeks of persuasion, Matt finally convinced the grocery store manager to let him take the aged produce to the local food pantry. The relationship with the grocery store manager continued to flourish and even after the trial period ended Matt was allowed to continue the program. Week after week, Matt transported the aged produce to the food pantry. Over time, the project grew and he needed additional hands. He then set up a relationship where another group would transport the food from the grocery store to the food pantry.

Six years later, his program saves 3-5 tons of food a month, enough to make 2,000 meals. Matt's creative solution created a symbiotic system which allows the discards of some to feed the mouths of others. When we use our creativity to create relationships where none existed previously, we allow others to benefit exponentially.

Think outside of the box 10% more often.

Find 10% more creative solutions.

Act on your ideas 10% more.

In a synergistic way,

through the power of 10%,

our actions can impact

the lives of many.

Sometimes creativity just means the daily work

of helping others to see a problem

in a different way.

~Joseph Badaracco

Creativity is the ability

to see relationships where none exist.

~Thomas Disch

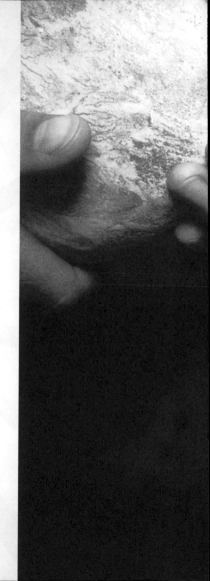

Purpose

The way you get meaning into your life is to
devote yourself to loving others,
devote yourself to your community around you,
and devote yourself to creating something
that gives you purpose and meaning.

~Mitch Albom

Some have called it
our nation's greatest injustice:
the inequity that exists in education
along socioeconomic and racial lines.

And one organization has made it their mission to "build the movement to eliminate educational inequity by enlisting our nation's most promising future leaders in the effort."

Teach For America began as an idea for Wendy Kopp's Princeton University thesis. She put her plan into action and in 1990, 500 men and women began teaching under the program in six low-income communities. Currently, there are 29 communities served, and more than 6,000 corps members, 14,000 alumni, and over 400,000 students impacted annually. Nearly 3 million students have been reached since they began. They have become the nation's largest provider of teachers for disadvantaged communities and have been recognized for being committed to educational equality and excellence.

Not only are current Teach For America corps members making a big impact, but alumni are as well. Thousands of Teach For America alumni are still teaching. More than 250 are principals of schools in disadvantaged communities. They are founders of education reform organizations, are serving on school boards, and are advising senators and governors on education policy.

Through the multiplier effect, the power of 10% has allowed one idea, which began in the mind of one woman, to become a powerful force to deal with a nationwide challenge. When many caring individuals come together for one purpose, the effects can be far-reaching.

How can you turn your ideas into action?

How can you make a difference?

How can you fulfill your purpose?

The purpose of human life is

to serve and to show compassion

and the will to help others.

~Albert Schweitzer

Great opportunities to help others seldom come,

but small ones surround us every day.

~Sally Koch

Giving

Sometimes when we are generous in small, barely detectable ways it can change someone else's life forever.

~Margaret Cho

Some call it *giving back*. Others call it *paying it forward*. Since 1991, we've called it *People Serving the Community*, or Project PSC. At The WALK THE TALK Company, one of our key corporate values is honoring our community and the world we live in; showing true appreciation for our success by helping those organizations that are helping others. Project PSC is a program through which each employee is provided with a year-end fund to contribute to the charitable service organization of his or her choice. The total amount that is dispersed throughout our community is 10% of the money allocated for our company's profit sharing program.

Over the years, we've contributed to scores of humanitarian organizations, such as food pantries, medical research charities, children's hospitals, and reading programs. Our 10% giving, combined with the donations of others, allows our efforts to be multiplied to truly make an impact.

The newspaper articles written about Project PSC have been kind. Receiving The Outstanding Volunteer of the Year Award was memorable. But what has touched our hearts, and has propelled us to continue the project for 17 straight years (even during times when our own company took a few financial hits), are the responses that we've gotten from the many organizations and individuals that have received our donations. The letters that we have received show us that we have made a difference in the lives of others. Over the years, we've read phrases such as:

IT IS ONLY THROUGH DONATIONS
LIKE YOURS THAT WE ARE ABLE TO
CONTINUE TO CARE FOR THOSE
WHO DESPERATELY NEED US.

Your gift of love and compassion allows
our residents to be warm and safe while
they rebuild their families and their lives.

Community support is
vital for our success.

Companies like yours are the critical
link to our continued existence.

With your help, we have saved thousands
of children from lives on the street.

Those are the words we love to hear.
This is why we do what we do.
There *is* power in giving.

When we give of ourselves, we can truly bless others.

Gifts, once given, alter the recipients' current realities and give them hope for a brighter future. The gift can be as simple as the warmth of a smile, a piece of sage advice, or the reassurance of friendship. The gift of compassion or empathy can lift the spirits of those who are hurt or distressed. The giving of our time, money, or talents can not only affect the hearts of those we give to, but can more tangibly improve their living conditions, economic status, and sense of security and stability.

Winston Churchill said, "We make a living by what we get, but we make a life by what we give." And it was Saint Francis of Assisi who said, "For it is in giving that we receive." Commit to giving 10% more than you do now. Give 10% more of your time, give 10% more of your resources, give 10% more of yourself. It is in this giving that we believe you will reap the satisfaction and joy of knowing that you have touched the hearts and lives of those around you.

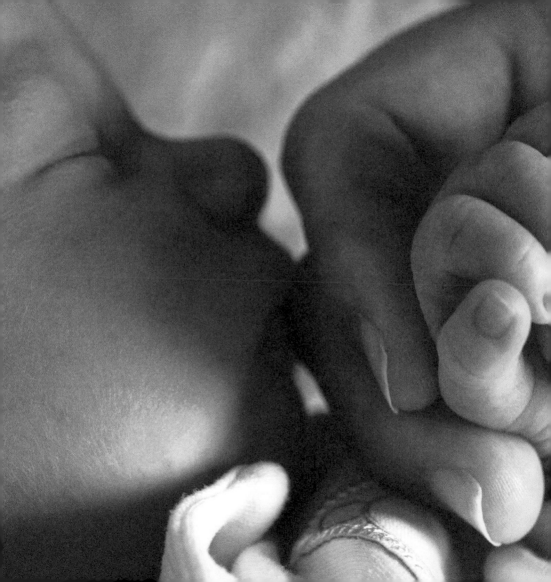

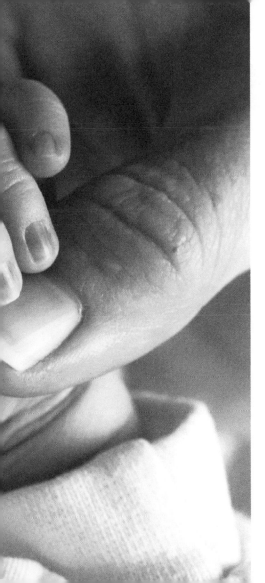

It's important to give it all you have while you have the chance.

~Shania Twain

One

We must remember that one determined person
can make a significant difference,
and that a small group of determined people
can change the course of history.

~Sonia Johnson

In 1996, she was awarded the Presidential Medal of Freedom.

In 1999, she received the Congressional Gold Medal of Honor.

In 2005, after she passed away, she became the first woman in American history to lie in state at the Capitol, an honor usually reserved for Presidents of the United States.

But on December 1, 1955, she was an unknown seamstress who refused to give up her bus seat to a white passenger.

Some consider Rosa Parks' courageous choice to stay seated to be the beginning of the modern day civil rights movement. By making a stand against injustice, she was arrested and tried for civil disobedience. This event sparked the Montgomery Bus Boycott and introduced the nation to Martin Luther King, Jr. In a later interview, Rosa said that at the moment of her arrest, she did not have any idea of how the people would react. Yet, through the power of 10%, her one small decision eventually led to the end of legal segregation in America. The small things *do* make a *very* big difference.

We must become the change we want to see.

~ Mahatma Gandhi

During difficulties, people often look at their circumstances and feel that they have no power to change things. Usually, they will either complain, or simply *do nothing*. Just as it only takes one candle to illuminate the darkness, those solitary individuals who choose to *do something* become instruments of change.

You may feel that your actions don't matter. You may feel that you can't possibly make a difference. You may feel that it is pointless to try to improve things. But, you are *one*. All that is needed to change the world is *one person* taking action.

As we take the first step, we set the wheels of change into motion. By doing what is right, standing up for our beliefs, and speaking out, we make the world a better place. Be a light for others so that they can become inspired to improve the world around them.

As we let our own light shine,

we unconsciously give other people

permission to do the same.

~Marianne Williamson

It is from numberless diverse acts

of courage and belief

that human history is shaped.

Each time a man stands up for an ideal,

or acts to improve the lot of others,

or strikes out against injustice,

he sends forth a tiny ripple of hope.

~Robert F. Kennedy

Closing Thoughts

As the ripple produced by the rock thrown into the still lake
expands into ever increasing concentric circles,
so do the effects of our power of 10% actions.

One idea, which is acted upon,
can change us and those around us
in *unimaginable* ways.

In order for you to conquer your fears, arrive at your destination, or achieve your dreams, you must take the first step. You do not need to see the end of the road in order to begin the journey.

Choose one 10% idea.
Hold that idea in your heart.
Reflect upon it.
Cultivate it.
And take action.

Just begin and unleash...

The Power of 10%

You've just discovered
The Power of 10%...

How Small Changes
Can Make a Big Difference

Let The Power of 10% now allow you to…

realize   that by removing your self-imposed boundaries, you open yourself up to limitless possibilities.

develop   a mindset that will give you courage to go after your goals, rather than to feel overwhelmed by them.

believe   that it's the small things that make a big difference.

improve   yourself and the world around you.

Best Wishes on Your Life's Journey,

Eric and Michelle

How wonderful it is that nobody

need wait a single moment

before starting to improve the world.

~Anne Frank

Introducing FREE online newsletters from WalkTheTalk.com

◆ **212° Monday Morning Must Read** — Monday morning motivation inspiring you to achieve results beyond your wildest expectations.

◆ **The Power of Inspiration** — Designed to uplift, inspire, and motivate you and the important people in your life.

◆ **Daily Motivation** — Powerful messages to "kick start" your day.

◆ **Leadership Lessons** — Weekly tips to help you and your colleagues become more effective and respected leaders.

◆ **Inspired Living** — Stretch your mind, nourish your soul, gladden your heart!

WalkTheTalk.com newsletters are designed to motivate, inform, and inspire you to reach new levels of skills and confidence.

Visit WalkTheTalk.com and sign up today!

To order additional copies of *The Power of 10%,* (only $12.95) visit WalkTheTalk.com

Better yet, order the *The Power of 10%* Inspirational Kit!

The Kit contains 5 powerful resources:

- ◆ The Power of 10% Book
- ◆ The Power of 10% Inspirational Movie
- ◆ The Power of 10% Motivational Screen Saver
- ◆ The Power of 10% Printable Poster
- ◆ The Power of 10% Personal Action Worksheet

Only $29.95* per kit

For a FREE Preview of the Inspirational Movie, visit WalkTheTalk.com

*Quantity Discounts Available

About The Authors

ERIC HARVEY, president and founder of WalkTheTalk.com, is a leading expert on Ethics and Values-Based Practices. He is a renowned business consultant and the author of thirty highly acclaimed books – including the best-selling *WALK the TALK, Ethics4Everyone* and *The Leadership Secrets of Santa Claus*. He and his team of professionals have helped thousands of individuals and organizations turn their values into value-added results.

MICHELLE SEDAS is the author of the best-selling book *Welcome The Rain* and coauthor of *The Power of 10%*. She is the editor of twenty-two books, including *WALK the TALK* gift book and *212° the extra degree* gift book. As the Senior Contributor for WalkTheTalk.com's *Inspired Living* newsletter, Michelle writes on themes intended to *stretch your mind, nourish your soul, and gladden your heart!* You can find Michelle at www.michellesedas.com.

About The Publisher

Since 1977, The WALK THE TALK Company (WalkTheTalk.com) has helped individuals and organizations, worldwide, achieve success through Values-Based Practices. Our goal is both simple and straightforward: to provide you and your organization with high-impact resources for your personal and professional success!

We specialize in:

- ◆ How-To Handbooks and Support Material
- ◆ Inspirational Books and Movies
- ◆ Motivational Newsletters
- ◆ Resources for Inspired Living
- ◆ Group Training Programs
- ◆ Do-It-Yourself Training Resources
- ◆ 360° Feedback Processes
   And Much More!

Contact us to learn more: www.walkthetalk.com
info@walkthetalk.com
888.822.9255